Kailas and Becky Rao Present

THE RESTORATION OF A MASTERPIECE

THE HERMAN AND CLAUDIA UIHLEIN MANSION

Arthur F. Hastings

Copyright: © Kailas and Becky Rao

International Standard Book Number 0-9747088-0-1

Author and Photographer: Arthur F. Hastings

Art Director: Michael Lyons, Whitefish Bay, Wisconsin

Editors: Becky Rao, Holly Smith

Editorial Assistants: Ernst Ulrich Franzen, Richard E. Kinder, Jr.,

Kate Mewes, Tony Skucas

Copy Proofer: Mary Uihlein Cunningham

Researcher: Laxman Kailas

Color Separations: Sells Printing

Printing: Sells Printing, New Berlin, Wisconsin

Printed in the United States of America

First Printing: December, 2003

To our dear friend Art Hastings.

In addition, we dedicate this book to our parents,
Mr. and Mrs. Kailas Bonthia, and Mr. and Mrs. W.W. Lott.
Although they came from humble means, their love, care, and spiritual
guidance taught us that we could dare to dream,
and in doing so, we could reach the stars.

Also, Kailas recognizes his older brother, Kailas Sree Ramlu,
who played a key role in Kailas' educational and entrepreneurial guidance.

TOMMY G. THOMPSON

1987-2001

"Your remarkable restoration of the old Uihlein Mansion is to be commended. This beautiful historic landmark only adds to the beauty of the great State of Wisconsin."

The Honorable Tommy G. Thompson
Former Wisconsin Governor

TABLE OF CONTENTS

FOREWORD

Rarely does one have the opportunity to live in a work of art. It may sound strange to refer to a house as a work of art, but there is really no other way to describe this place—a home we have admired for so many years, a home that has become a local treasure.

When we purchased the house in 1993, we knew that to restore it was to save it for the future, to preserve it for generations to come. Because such great care had been taken in building the Uihlein Mansion in 1919, we believed that it was essential to show respect for those artisans and craftsmen who created this lovely Mansion and whose skills are still so obvious in the details they wrought in every room. We wanted the Mansion restored and maintained with the same care.

The restoration, a long and sometimes difficult process, took over three years, including six months of intensive research, and involved over sixty contractors. It was, however, a labor of love for us as we watched new life enter these stately rooms. Under the incredible leadership of Interior Designer Jon Schlagenhaft and Project Manager Gregory Pardo, a host of artists and craftsmen, all genuinely respectful of the rich history that is so apparent throughout this home, made our vision for this house a reality. We are fortunate to have the resources to create another chapter in the history of the Uihlein Mansion, and we are delighted to be able to share it with each of you.

Kailas and Becky Rao

HISTORY

Near the end of the 19th century, Captain Frederick Pabst of the Pabst Brewing Company built a magnificent resort on the shores of Lake Michigan five miles north of downtown Milwaukee—a clear signal that the battle of the "beer barons" had gone beyond the sale and distribution of beer. A few years earlier, the Uihleins, co-founders of the rival Jos. Schlitz Brewing Company, had built the Schlitz Palm Garden at the corner of Grand Avenue (now Wisconsin Avenue) and Third Street in downtown Milwaukee. At this elegant restaurant and refreshment hall, locals and celebrities alike sat beneath brightly lit vaulted ceilings, quenching their thirst with Schlitz beer.

After selecting 18 acres of spectacular lake bluff property in the rich farmland of Whitefish Bay, Captain Pabst built a 250-foot-long gingerbread-encrusted Atlantic City-style pavilion that housed lounging parlors, dining rooms, and a giant circular bar overlooking Lake Michigan. Seated inside at this grand bar or outside at any number of tables situated on the back patio, on benches beneath the trees, or at the mushroom-shaped tables positioned along the walkways that interlaced the bluff, patrons enjoyed a delightfully festive ambience while listening to band concerts and sipping Pabst's famous Blue Ribbon Beer. Only a few years after the resort opened, Pabst added yet another amusement to draw the paying public—a 50-foot Ferris wheel that towered at the northern end of the park where patrons lined up for the chance to claim one of ten passenger seats that circled the revolving wheel high above Lake Michigan.

The Whitefish Bay Resort attracted throngs of Milwaukeeans. Some came by horse and carriage along Lake Avenue; others arrived on either the *Bloomer Girl* or the *Eagle*, steamboats that traveled from the docks in downtown Milwaukee to the long passenger pier jutting out from the lakeshore just below the resort; others made the journey by train along a specially constructed "dummy line" that every 45 minutes carried passengers from downtown directly to the park's main gate.

With the turn of the century, the automobile, which allowed people to travel greater distances in less time, became increasingly popular. No longer content to limit their daytrips to the lake bluff acreage of the Pabst Whitefish Bay Resort, many Milwaukeeans began to take jaunts to more distant locales. At the same time, an increasing number of visitors to the Whitefish Bay Resort began to carry their own picnic lunches and beverages. The result of these trends was that Pabst's sales at the Whitefish Bay Resort began to dwindle. Subsequently, in 1914, the resort, which had once been Milwaukee's "furthest north," was closed; its buildings, razed.

By the following year, the newly platted Whitefish Bay Subdivision had replaced the once-famous Whitefish Bay Resort.

VISION OF A MASTERPIECE

Herman Uihlein was the son and heir of Henry Uihlein, president of Jos. Schlitz Brewing Company. In 1911 he married Claudia Holt, an aspiring opera singer in New York City and daughter of John Holt of Salt Lake City, Utah. That same year Herman, a graduate of Cornell University and former law student at Columbia University, was appointed president of the newly formed Lavine Gear Company. He also sat on the board of directors at the Schlitz Brewing Company. After her marriage to Herman, Claudia Uihlein, a former student of ballet and opera, continued to involve herself in the creative arts by serving as their patron.

When Herman and Claudia first toured the site of the former Pabst Whitefish Bay Resort in 1915, all that remained was random debris—a few scattered tables, fragments of walkways, remnants of the pier. Nevertheless, the spectacular natural beauty of the bluff land along Lake Michigan greatly impressed the Uihleins, and, shortly after their tour of the property, they became among the first to buy one of the newly available three-acre lots.

Mrs. Uihlein, who had traveled extensively in Europe, was keen to incorporate a number of European architectural elements and designs into the house she and Herman were having built. She spent a considerable amount of time looking at house designs until eventually she found one that seemed to have all the qualities she desired. She took this design to Thomas L. Rose of the architectural firm Kirchhoff & Rose, which had designed the enormously popular Schlitz Palm Garden.

Kirchhoff & Rose spent the next year and a half drawing up detailed blueprints — including a 134-page book on specifications—for the magnificent Italian Renaissance mansion that would become a showplace for scores of Old World craftsmen— masons, carpenters, electricians, ornamental plaster artists, glass and marble artisans.

One such artisan had been commissioned to design and create the extensive array of ironwork throughout the Mansion. The renowned ornamental ironwork artist Cyril Colnik had studied the craft in his native Vienna, Austria, as well as in other European countries. Colnik first came to the United States to work on the German exhibit at the 1893 Colombian Exposition World's Fair in Chicago. He later moved to Milwaukee to start his own business. By the early 20th century, Colnik had established himself as the leading ornamental ironwork craftsman in the city.

It is said to have taken Colnik over three years to design and forge all of the custom ironwork, including the ornamental iron entry doors, the stunning Grand Staircase balustrade, the indoor fountains, furniture, fireplace screens, chandeliers, sconces, torchères, fireplace tools, and the other equally impressive grilles and balcony railings.

In June 1919 when the Mansion was completed, the Uihlein family—Herman and Claudia and their three children, who would later be joined by four more children, including a set of twins—moved in. Drawing immediate national attention, the stunning Mansion merited a four-page picture story in the August 1920 issue of *Town Topics*, a magazine comparable to today's *Town & Country* or *Architectural Digest*.

Soon the Mansion was central to the Milwaukee social scene. Not only was it the site of frequent dinner parties, but it was also the setting for musicales, which were held every Sunday afternoon. On these occasions, the Aeolian two-manual pipe organ installed in the Grand Foyer served to showcase the talents of various nationally prominent organists who were regular visitors to the house, including Louis Vantine, organist of St. Patrick's Cathedral in New York City.

Over the years the Uihlein house accommodated a host of celebrities. Among these notable guests were Lillian Gish, Irene Dunne, Alma Peterson, Eddie Cantor, and Jack Benny. It was the Mansion itself however that drew the most notice. It was quite simply a masterpiece.

In constructing the Uihlein Mansion, not only did Kirchhoff & Rose create a splendid design, but they expertly matched the raw materials used in the home's construction to its Italian Renaissance architecture. The exterior of the Mansion was constructed of smooth, buff-colored Bedford limestone blocks extracted from a single layer within an Indiana quarry. All stone ornamentation was carved on site.

Cyril Colnik created the magnificent forged iron front entry doors and transom, both excellent examples of the craftsmanship found throughout the house. The entry doors were set within a rounded arch and screened by an elaborate scrolled and floriated wrought-iron grille. Above the entry, the second-story balcony rested on a richly carved limestone ancon and consoles. The wrought-iron balcony rail bore a stylized hop medallion symbolizing the brewing interests of the Uihlein family. French doors provided access to the balcony.

Inside the front doors, a set of exquisite hand-carved French walnut inner doors and a matching transom separated the vestibule from the Grand Foyer. The Italian Travertine marble walls of the vestibule complemented the three-marble parquet floor and the elaborate wrought-iron grilles.

For the Grand Staircase of the Grand Foyer, Colnik crafted a floriated wrought-iron balustrade whose consecutive panels were joined by intertwining vines and embellished with acanthus leaves and organic emblems. This balustrade was topped with a walnut handrail and mounted on Travertine marble steps. (The walnut handrail of the Grand Staircase was carved by the same craftsman who would carve the propeller for Charles Lindbergh's famed airplane, the *Spirit of St. Louis*, eight years later.) The staircase ascended to a landing before splitting into north and south flights leading to the second level. Installed just above the landing was a two-story Palladian window overlooking Lake Michigan.

Floriated wrought-iron torchères and wall sconces flanked the base of the staircase and the great window at the landing.

The Grand Foyer's ornate ceiling had a geometric pattern formed by ornamental plaster-coffered deep reliefs and crown moldings. Framed between two hand-carved walnut pocket doors was an Amherst sandstone Italian Renaissance-style fireplace mantel, which had carved into its center a gargoyle that, according to Austrian belief, would ward off "evil spirits" if set near the entrance of the house. The parquet floor of the Grand Foyer was inlaid with three marbles—Travertine, Breccia Damascota, and Red Levant—set in a diamond checkerboard design. The Red Levant marble was used repeatedly throughout the Mansion, particularly in the baseboards and fireplace surrounds. Accenting the Foyer floor was a beautiful rose red area rug.

On both sides of the entrance door were ornately carved closet doors, which, like all of the woodwork of the Grand Foyer, had been carved by the Matthews Brothers woodworking firm. Behind one door was a cloak closet; behind the other, the Aeolian two-manual pipe organ and console. The carved French walnut organ grilles above the closets were some of the finest examples of wood-carving artistry of the era. The Foyer walls were made of fine-grained yellow Caen limestone imported from northern France.

Off the Grand Foyer in the southwest corner of the Mansion lay the Drawing Room. Designed in Louis XV style, this room was fashioned after a parlor in the Palace of Versailles near Paris, France. The centerpiece of the Drawing Room was the carved marble fireplace mantel flanked by fine crystal chandeliers. The handcrafted crystal chandeliers highlighted two rare Chinese vases that sat on top of a fine old Louis XV table in the center of the room. A large Savonnerie-style rug covered the floor.

Rising from the floor to the ceiling was an arcade of round-topped Palladian windows framed by peach and gold brocade window draperies with gold taffeta draw curtains, which contrasted with the room's pale gray walls. The furniture was upholstered with richly colored silk brocade and Aubusson tapestry. A large, lush polar bear rug was spread out before the marble fireplace. Detailed ornamental plasterwork, including crown moldings and plaster filigree, embellished the ornate Drawing Room ceiling.

To the east of the Drawing Room, the less formal but equally beautiful Garden Room overlooked Lake Michigan. In this room where the Uihlein family relaxed, Palladian windows to the south and the east allowed in light, color, and warmth from the morning sun. French doors provided exits to two separate terraces on the south and east sides of the room.

The Garden Room featured furniture upholstered with printed linens. The cushions of the wrought-iron sofa and easy chairs were covered with cream and mauve fabrics. Painted murals depicting Venetian garden scenes, including a colonnade of Roman-style statues, adorned the upper half of the Garden Room walls. Two matched marble and iron indoor water fountains, wrought by Cyril Colnik, were positioned at the room's southern end.

Across the Great Hall to the north were the Dining Room, Library, and Kitchen. The luxurious Dining Room was a reproduction of the banquet room of Forde Abbey, in Chard, Somerset, England. Paneled in French walnut, its walls featured exquisitely carved molding, wainscoting, crown molding, and capital-topped columns. A splendid example of artistic plaster design, the Dining Room ceiling possessed an outer border of acanthus leaves with wreaths of fruit adorning each corner and an inner border of sunflowers, acorns, and oak leaves.

Covering the Dining Room floor was a soft blue, ivory, and gold hand-tufted Irish rug that repeated the pattern of the ornamental plaster ceiling above it. On the windows were draperies of blue and gold damask. An antique French console served as a buffet. A multi-hued green Flemish tapestry screen was suspended between the Dining Room and the adjoining Butler's Pantry. At the center of the room stood a massive wooden table and chairs, above which hung a German sterling silver chandelier. When the Uihlein children dined with their parents, their small walnut caned chairs were placed among the larger chairs.

The English Jacobean-style Library was located across the hall from the Dining Room. Its quarter-sawn white oak-paneled walls were framed by carved molding and highlighted by an ornately carved oak fireplace mantel. Flanking the fireplace were exquisitely carved oak pilasters upon which lost wax-casting wall sconces were mounted. A matching chandelier was suspended above the center of the room.

Green damask draperies, highlighted with subtle purple tones, framed the Library windows. Furnishings covered in green, orange, and red-toned fabrics and a green rug were reminiscent of the English countryside.

The Kitchen, designed to accommodate food preparation for not only intimate family dinners but also large banquets, featured state-of-the-art appliances, including built-in refrigerators and electric and gas stoves. Between the Kitchen and Dining Room was the Butler's Pantry, which housed a built-in plate-warming cabinet, a German nickel silver sink, and countertops of pink Tennessee marble.

Because eating in the Kitchen and the Pantry was forbidden, a small separate children's dining area was built off the west end of the Kitchen. The table and chairs in this dining area were specifically designed to stand higher than standard so that the staff were able to attend to the children's needs without straining their backs.

The Grand Staircase and the Servants' Stairway provided access to the family quarters. On the second story of the Mansion were nine bedrooms—five for the family and four for the servants—and four bathrooms—three for the family and one for the servants. Three of the servants' bedrooms had wall-hung lavatories.

The family bedrooms and bathrooms were connected by doorways that ran along the entire western wall of the Mansion; thus, the bedroom farthest from the Master Suite was only a series of doors away, giving the parents access to their children without their entering the main hallway.

The Master Suite included a nursery, a Boudoir, and the Master Bedroom, which had ivory-colored walls with striped silk lampas curtains and contained dark walnut twin beds covered with the same pale rose fabric used for the curtains.

Mrs. Uihlein's Boudoir, with its blue and silver damask walls framed by ivory-painted wood molding and its pink taffeta brocade drapes, was filled with rose, blue, and gold brocade-covered furniture and featured oil paintings of roses on canvas mounted over the doorways.

Here in this Mansion by the Lake, the Uihlein family lived and flourished for nearly a quarter of a century.

Nevertheless, at more than 60 years, the house was inevitably showing its age. The Mansion remained impressive, but it was in need of extensive repair. Because they were nearing retirement, the Beutners eventually decided to sell the Mansion and move to a smaller house. Thus, in 1987, Steven and Christiana Nicolet became owners of the Mansion, purchasing it for $550,000. Within two years, however, the Nicolets had sold the Mansion and relocated to nearby Fox Point.

Two years later, Peter and Mary Buffett of San Francisco walked through the house. Upon entering the foyer of the grand old Mansion, the Buffets knew that, despite its enormous size, they wanted to make the Mansion their home. Consequently, they bought the house for $1.175 million, which was at that time the highest price ever recorded for a private residence in this elegant North Shore community. The Buffetts, like the Uihleins and Buetners, entertained numerous guests. They also used the Mansion to house their music production company, Independent Sound.

During the Buffetts' residency in the Mansion, a fully synthesized recording studio was installed on the third floor, and musicians from all over the country came to record commercial musical scores. Attracting musicians to the house was an easy task, for most musicians preferred to play in the beautiful surroundings provided by the Mansion rather than in a sterile sound studio.

In 1992, the Buffetts decided to place the Mansion on the market. On moving day, a huge crane appeared at the house to pluck the 900-pound audio board from the third-floor portico porch, thereby ending yet another chapter in the history of the Uihlein Mansion.

Over the next year, many potential buyers were paraded through the Mansion. The asking price was $1.751 million.

REVISION OF A MASTERPIECE

For years, Kailas and Becky Rao had driven past the Mansion on their way to and from their modest home farther north in Whitefish Bay. Like countless other passersby, they felt both awed and inspired when they looked at this magnificent Mansion on the Lake.

From its construction, the Mansion had always had a certain magnetism. Anyone passing by the estate would inevitably be drawn to its broad lawn and to the elegant Mansion that crowned it. Most admired the Mansion from the sidewalk; others, more daring, would drive slowly around its circular drive, imagining and, perhaps, asking themselves one question: what would it be like to live in such a grand house?

For Kailas and Becky Rao, this question was not merely the product of wishful thinking. The Raos not only wanted to make the old Mansion their home, they also wanted to restore and preserve it for the community that had given them so much. They envisioned for their community a unique and long-lasting gift. By restoring the Mansion, the Raos would not only be preserving an architectural masterpiece, a monument to Old World craftsmanship and to the Uihlein's original vision, they would also be preserving a part of their community's illustrious history. For the Raos, this gift they envisioned could indeed become a reality.

Years before, while working as an assistant professor of accounting in the School of Business at the University of Wisconsin-Milwaukee, Kailas had seen an opportunity to participate in the fledgling personal computer industry. In 1980, he founded a personal computer center named Computers Unlimited of Wisconsin Inc., which provided value-added services (VARS) to businesses.

Over the next three years, the Raos were successful in opening additional computer centers in the greater Milwaukee area. Eventually, these computer centers were franchised, and Computers Unlimited evolved into Computer Bay, a franchisor of personal computer equipment, whose franchisees grew to 350 centers in 44 states. Then, in 1992, Kailas and Becky sold Computer Bay. Proceeds from the sale provided them with the means to purchase the Uihlein Mansion and, thus, fulfill a long-held dream. Negotiations went on for three months. It was clear that the restoration costs would greatly exceed the asking price; indeed, a number of the Raos' associates cautioned them against buying the Mansion. Despite these warnings, however, the Raos were determined to purchase it.

In June 1993, Peter Buffett accepted the Raos' offer of $1.3 million.

The first major obstacle encountered by the restoration team was the leaking roof. Previously, the roofing contractor had projected a budget based on his inspection of the areas of the attic where leaking had occurred. He had even broken through the ceilings in several places to check the rafters and the underside of the roof. However, a short time later, workers accidentally discovered that what appeared to be the underside of the roof was actually a sub-roof placed midway between the ceilings and the actual roof. When they pulled away a section of the sub-roof, they found that the entire underside of the roof had rotted and would need to be replaced. In some areas, the roof had to be completely removed. Steel beams were installed to ensure structural integrity. Almost immediately, the roof budget tripled.

At the same time, Edward E. Gillen & Company, contractors specializing in foundations and piers, began delivering 800 metric tons of armor stone, which was strategically placed in front of the old seawall at the base of the bluff. A procession of trucks—more than 600 in all—made its way to the Mansion week after week until the shoreline was stabilized and the seawall was protected from erosion.

Inside the Mansion, electricians began the task of rewiring each room, beginning in the sub-basement utility rooms and working their way up. Every wire was replaced; the fuse boxes were removed; circuit breakers were installed; outlets were added; the chandeliers and sconces were removed, rewired, and restored. During this rewiring, the 400-amp service was upgraded to 800 amps, and provisions were made to accommodate new telephone, security, cable, and satellite systems. In total, approximately five miles of electrical wire was installed.

When the electricians completed their work in each room, the carpenters would begin theirs, removing walls, old insulation, unusable cabinets, flooring and tile; painting contractors stripped paint from walls, floors, ceilings, and moldings. In some places, up to 15 layers of paint were removed. For each of the rooms being remodeled, ornamental plaster artist Paul Casey repaired the original plaster and cast new ornamental plaster, as necessary.

When it became clear that the original windows were not salvageable, all 174 doors and windows were replaced, because it would be more energy efficient and less costly. Each new door and window, including the two-story Palladian window at the staircase landing of the Grand Foyer, was designed to replicate the one it replaced. The Kitchen and the Butler's Pantry were gutted. All nine bathrooms were dismantled. Their gray and white tiles, typical of the early 1900s, and plumbing fixtures, pipes, and lavatories were removed. All iron and lead piping was replaced with PVC and copper; all asbestos was removed.

With the new roof and most of the windows replaced by mid-summer 1994, the renovation of the interior began in earnest. By this point, the extensive redesigning of the landscape also had begun. Indeed, every square foot of the estate had become a construction zone. Every day by 7:00 a.m., various trucks and vans transported an army of craftsmen to the Mansion.

Inside the Mansion, craftsmen were not only bringing the place up to code, they were bringing new life into every corner. Outside, workers were excavating the front lawn in order to replace all utility lines from the street to the Mansion. A water main, storm drain, sewer line, natural gas line, electrical, telephone, and television cables were laid in deep trenches.

A 90-foot-long reflection pool and fountain were installed on the front lawn, and new circular driveways were installed. In the center of the backyard, a brick lawn terrace was laid, and a new retaining wall separating the formal gardens from the bluff was constructed.

THE GRAND FOYER

The Grand Foyer, the heart of the Mansion, was one of the first rooms to get a complete makeover. The Foyer's Caen limestone walls were chemically treated to bring back their pale bisque hue. The marble floors were stripped, ground, and polished to restore their original luster. The coffered plaster ceiling was stripped of old paint, repaired, painted, glazed, and gold leafed.

The wrought-iron balustrade of the Grand Staircase was sandblasted with black sand and painted. Its walnut banister was stripped and re-varnished. The Travertine marble stairs were also stripped and polished, and hand-loomed carpeting in gold wool with a deep red border replicating the acanthus leaf pattern found in the balustrade was laid on the staircase.

Uihlein family photographs of the original chandelier were used as a guide in creating the magnificent wrought-iron chandelier that was forged for the center of the Grand Foyer. The intricately designed, hand-carved Amherst sandstone fireplace mantel was cleaned and repaired, and the hand-forged fireplace tools, screen and irons were refurbished.

The hand-carved French walnut doors, moldings, organ grilles, and interior transom were stripped and refinished.

When the restoration work in the Grand Foyer was completed, elegant antique furnishings were added. Placed on the north wall is a 19th-century antique French Boule chest inlaid with brass and red tortoise shell and featuring

handsome brass door mountings. Above the chest is a mid-19th-century French rococo mirror. Hanging nearby from a wrought-iron dowel rod, a beautiful 19th-century French tapestry depicts a typical French pastoral scene with hunters on horseback, hounds, and a damsel in distress.

A staircase off the Grand Foyer provides access to the lower level and features a cream-colored damask wall covering designed and printed by renowned San Francisco artists Mark Evans and Charley Brown. The Scalamandré trompe l'oeil ceiling paper used in the lower foyer creates the illusion of a coffered ceiling.

THE FORMAL LIVING ROOM

Adjacent to the Grand Foyer on the southwest end of the Mansion is the Formal Living Room. The original teak floor is laid out in classic Versailles-style parquetry. A large grate in the floor was replaced with matching teak panels, refinished to match the original flooring, and the entire floor was hand-waxed to restore its original splendor.

Because the original carved plaster mirror was missing from above the Living Room fireplace mantel, a new plaster mirror, replicating the stylistic embellishments of the original, was created by Paul Casey and then permanently mounted over the fireplace.

The original fireplace mantel and chandeliers had been missing from the Living Room since the 1940s. Consequently, Schlagenhaft, using family photos provided by Mary Uihlein Cunningham, tracked down, acquired, and installed pieces from a New York City antique dealer. The new pieces were almost identical to the originals—a French carved Italian Carrara marble mantel and Louis XV Baccarat crystal chandeliers.

The Drawing Room, also known as the Music Room and Ladies' Parlor, was patterned after a drawing room in the Palace of Versailles. During the restoration, countless coats of paint were removed, the plaster ornamentation was repaired, and the walls and ceilings were painted and glazed. The plasterwork was then masterfully leafed in 23.5-karat gold by Conrad Schmitt Studios.

Louis XV furnishings sit on a large hand-loomed rug, its design similar to that of a rug found in the Palace of Versailles. More than one year was required to handloom this rug, which incorporates over 65 colors of yarn in its French Aubusson floral pattern.

Although there were no wall sconces in the Drawing Room when the restoration began, the Mansion's original blueprints indicated that wall sconces were to be hung between each window in the Drawing Room and on either side of the Foyer entrance doors. When holes were drilled at these sites, exactly where indicated on the blueprints, not surprisingly, electrical boxes were found. These electrical boxes were rewired, and today six matching Baccarat crystal sconces hang, as originally intended.

Two chairs original to the house have been re-upholstered and re-gilded, and original table lamps flank the oversized antique French sofa. A parlor grand piano (circa 1926) graces the corner of the room where Claudia Uihlein's piano once stood. The hand-sewn, Italian-made Scalamandré silk woven damask draperies replicate the window treatments depicted in original photographs.

THE TERRACE ROOM

In the southeast corner of the Mansion next to the Formal Living Room, the Terrace Room overlooks Lake Michigan to the east and the formal garden to the south. With windows and French doors on three sides, this room seemed the perfect place to install murals depicting the countryside of India, Kailas Rao's homeland. To achieve this goal, the room was first stripped of all paint and existing wall coverings. New French doors and windows were then installed.

Mark Evans and Charley Brown, who specialize in the art of trompe l'oeil painting, created exquisite ceiling murals of deep blue skies, puffy white clouds, and billowing blue-and-white-striped banners, images reminiscent of Becky Rao's first impressions of India. Indian pastoral scenes of mosques and temples, images of the Taj Mahal, elephants at a watering pond, a white Bengal tiger, and India's national bird, the peacock, are also depicted on the Terrace Room walls.

53

Two wrought-iron and marble Cyril Colnik water fountains, refitted with new circulation pumps and plumbing, stand spaced between the three Terrace doors of the room's south wall. The Terrace Room's Verde marble fireplace mantel, baseboards, and Travertine marble floor were also restored.

Surrounded by palm trees and floral arrangements, an ivory damask-covered French sofa and matching chairs are positioned around a hand-carved marble table inlaid in semi-precious stones from Agra, India. Flanking the fireplace are two semi-circular wrought-iron and marble Cyril Colnik tables. Herman Uihlein, Jr. had graciously presented these tables to the Raos when the restoration of the Mansion was completed.

THE DINING ROOM

Having been impressed with the dining hall of the Forde Abbey in Chard, Somerset, England during her travels, Claudia Uihlein had recreated this striking room in her Whitefish Bay house. When she sold the Mansion in the late 1940s, the original paneling, woodwork, and carved limestone fireplace were removed for future use in another house. However, the paneling, which had been stored in a warehouse for a number of years, was subsequently lost.

Fortunately, archival photographs and old blueprints enabled master craftsmen from World of Wood, Ltd. to restore the Dining Room, which is situated across from the Grand Foyer to the northeast, to its original grandeur.

To restore the Dining Room paneling, veneers from a single American black walnut tree were chosen. When this paneling was installed around the room, the grained cathedral patterns were perfectly book-matched. Twelve separate walnut moldings were crafted and installed along with the fireplace mantel, which was hand-carved from Bedford, Indiana limestone and inlaid with Red Levanto marble. The ornate plaster ceiling was stripped of numerous coats of paint to reveal a wealth of floral reliefs, birds, sunflowers, acorns, oak leaves, and floral wreaths. The artists painstakingly "antiqued" and porcelain-glazed the ceiling. The German-made silver chandelier that had originally hung above the Uihlein dining table was cleaned, lacquered, rewired, and hangs once more in the center of the Dining Room.

After the marble floor and baseboards were polished, a new hand-loomed replica of the original area rug, which mirrors the design of the ornamental plaster ceiling above it, was installed. A 12-foot-long replica of an antique English dining table, crafted from a single piece of walnut and bordered with inlaid satin wood, provides formal seating for 14 dinner guests. Standing against the south wall, a marvelous Italian-made, Beidermier-style china cabinet from Columbo Stile showcases Faberge porcelain china and Baccarat Malmaison crystal. Also included in this collection are a crystal vase from Mosser Co. of Prague, gold-lined sterling silver goblets from Malaysia, and Wedgewood Jasperware from England.

When the Dining Room restoration was completed, Mary Uihlein Cunningham generously gave the Raos the six caned chairs that she and her siblings had used when, as children, they were allowed to join their parents for dinner.

The Library

L ocated across the hallway from the Dining Room on the northwestern corner of the Mansion is the Library, its two Palladian windows facing west.

Originally stained in dark oak typical of the English Jacobean style, the quarter-sawn white oak paneling, pilasters, and elaborate moldings were stripped, bleached, and refinished in a lighter color to brighten up the dark room. The Library floor was completely redone with new tongue-and-groove oak strips in a herringbone pattern.

The hand-carved sandstone fireplace mantel was cleaned and repaired. The original bronze lost wax-cast chandelier and matching wall sconces flanking the fireplace were cleaned, rewired, and re-hung. A Charley Brown oil painting depicting Becky Rao's horses, "Horses of a Life-Time," was installed in a panel over the fireplace, and two glass front gun cases were installed in the north wall to showcase her collection of antique shotguns.

Included among the furnishings are an English Regency reproduction desk resting on gold-leaf-detailed ebony carved griffin legs, a large brown Queen Anne leather sofa, and a black lacquer Chinese cabinet with chinoiserie appliqué.

THE POWDER ROOM

The small Powder Room was recreated in a stunning gold palette. Its unique groin-arched vaulted ceiling was made possible when carpenters removed pipe organ chambers that were located above the original ceiling. Beneath this gold-leafed domed ceiling are a tiger-eye veneer vanity with a 24-karat gold-plated washbasin and tiger-eye faucets, and wall sconces created by Sherle Wagner of New York. An antique chandelier hangs at the apex of the groin vault and an antique mirror hangs above the basin. Bright gold and brown palm tree-patterned wall coverings adorn the walls. Its floor was retiled with genuine tiger-eye and dark taupe and brown Saint Laurent marble.

The Game Room

The Game Room, once the children's eating area, had long ago been converted into a smoking parlor by Herman Uihlein, and doors were cut into the south wall to provide a passageway into the Library. In the 1930s, a small Art Deco bar had been added.

Today the Game Room reflects a passion for hunting. The room features an eight-sided silver-leafed domed ceiling covered in a specially designed Evans & Brown trompe l'oeil mural, which depicts outdoor vignettes of game typically hunted in Wisconsin—duck, pheasant, deer and wild turkey. Set into an arching octagonal design and framed in magenta, gold, brown, and azure blue are alternating sepia-toned painted vignettes depicting hunting dogs, past and present.

The same quarter-sawn white oak moldings and pilasters found in the Library
also highlight the Game Room walls, which are covered in embossed leather.
The Game Room's herringbone-patterned tongue-and-groove oak floor,
continued from the Library, is covered by a deep red hand-woven area rug
designed in a Greek key pattern by Savnik & Co. An antique English chandelier
decorated with bronze elk heads holding crystal baskets in their mouths is
suspended over the antique, leather-topped game table. Surrounding this table
are antique serpentine-leg chairs.

The wet bar originally installed by Herman Uihlein was enlarged and modernized
to include an icemaker and a refrigerator. Brown granite countertops were installed
to complement the Brunschwig & Fils antique tapestry wallpaper. An arched
pass-through outfitted with sliding beaded-glass windows was cut into the wall
facing the hall.

THE KITCHEN AND BUTLER'S PANTRY

During the renovation, the Kitchen and Butler's Pantry were combined to create a cooking center suitable for professional caterers' use or for quiet family kitchen eat-ins. The Kitchen table's white marble top is inlaid with hand-cut semi-precious stones arranged in a floral pattern. This exquisite tabletop, created by artists commissioned in India, sits on a wrought-iron base. Suspended over the table is a Cyril Colnik brass and iron chandelier, which originally hung in the Terrace Room.

The cabinets are framed in hard rock maple complemented by birds eye maple door fronts. In the former Butler's Pantry area, the maple cabinets feature leaded glass door fronts made of clear German seeded tavern glass. The uniquely patterned hardware throughout this room is hand-forged iron.

The Kitchen includes the only visible structural change made to the Mansion during its renovation. A large window on the east wall was replaced with French doors that lead to a 16-foot-square elevated terrace. This terrace, which during the summer months is frequently used for outdoor dining, provides a panoramic view of Lake Michigan.

Rare Brazilian blue bahia granite, selected by Schlagenhaft, was used for all of the countertops throughout the Kitchen and Butler's Pantry. To ensure consistency of pattern and color, this striking blue granite was taken from a single layer within one quarry. Because matching the color of the granite from any subsequent cuts would have been virtually impossible, tremendous care was taken during the measuring of the countertops. Colorful hand-painted Portuguese tiles bearing a delightful French culinary motif function as the backsplash.

The archway between the Kitchen and Butler's Pantry is decorated by a pair of Barley Twist style wooden columns faux-painted by Milwaukee artist Paul Mandracchia to match the blue granite of the Kitchen and Butler's Pantry countertops.

The Kitchen renovation included the installation of an ice-maker, a dishwasher, warming drawers, a three cook top gourmet cooking island, a grill, matching built-in Gaggenau ovens, a Sub-Zero refrigerator, double sinks, a bar sink, and an instant hot water faucet.

The hallway leading from the Kitchen to the Grand Foyer, originally intended for servants' use, has been transformed into a more formal space. As in the Grand Foyer, the floors are Travertine and Red Levanto Marble. New oak moldings match the elegant wood paneling of the nearby Library and Game Room. The walls are covered in a Clarence House French toile depicting *The Marriage of Figaro*. Hanging in the hallway are a pair of matching Cyril Colnik chandeliers with electric sockets and gas jets. The rear stairs leading to the living quarters on the second floor are covered with a navy blue and gold English Axminster carpet.

UPPER FOYER

An Evans & Brown trompe l'oeil mural, reminiscent of 17th-century baroque ceiling panels found in many palaces and churches in Europe, was installed on the Upper Foyer ceiling. The scene depicted on this mural represents the triumph of civilization (the muses of Art, Truth, Poetry, Geometry, Architecture, and Music) over the forces of evil (Ignorance, Injustice, and Brutality). An Evans & Brown-designed painted architectural cornice, which repeats the intricate floral and leaf design found in the iron balustrade of the staircase, frames the mural.

The Master Suite is at the south end of the upper hallway. To the north are the President's Suite, other guest rooms, and the Media Room, a private living room for the Raos. A single piece of furniture is showcased in the Upper Foyer—a massive antique French Boule credenza inlaid with brass and bronze designs of

birds, animals, flowers, and muses. Displayed upon this credenza is a 19th-century Viennese porcelain urn featuring a portrait of Alexander the Great. A pair of antique cast bronze sculptures of vines, wheat spikes, grape bunches, and flowers are positioned on each side of the urn. Matching crystal sconces echo the Baccarat chandelier in the Grand Staircase.

THE MASTER SUITE

The Master Suite comprises three rooms and a hallway with a single entrance. Originally, a nursery with a separate doorway adjoined the Master Bath and hallway. During renovation, the doorway to this nursery was permanently sealed, and a large Master Bathroom with its own foyer, shower room, water closet, whirlpool spa tub and matching marble

vanities was installed. Both the original main hallway closets with built-in dressers and those in the Boudoir were

removed. A new double-door entry was made in the center of the hallway allowing direct passage from the Boudoir to the Master Bathroom. Doorways between the hallway and Master Bedroom and the Boudoir and the Master Bedroom were left intact; however, the doorway between the Boudoir and the adjacent President's Suite was permanently walled off to create greater privacy.

A handmade Tiffany-style stained-glass panel created by the Schlitz Art Glass
Studio of Milwaukee replaced the hallway's original clear glass skylight. The
colors of this masterfully designed panel include the same vivid pinks and greens
found in the Brunschwig & Fils trellis-garden arcade wall covering in the hallway
and in the hand-loomed wool Louis XV-style carpeting throughout the suite.

THE MASTER BATH

The Master Bath is designed in a symmetrical picture-frame pattern reflecting the stately elegance of the suite. The Master Bath foyer features a pink and white Venetian glass chandelier original to the Mansion. Three kinds of marble adorn the floors: white Greek Thassos, pink Norwegian Rose, and green Verde Antique. The foyer has all three colors of marble set in a square plane. The bath area includes all three colors set diagonally. The water closet is tiled in white and pink marble. The shower is made with white marble and trimmed in pink.

The Master Bath includes a raised Kallista whirlpool tub set on a marble base, with tub surround and vanities made of pink Norwegian Rose marble. The steam shower has gold-plated body jets. The toilet and bidet are hand-painted in a floral pattern by Sherle Wagner. Louis XV-style vanities are topped by matching Sherle Wagner Greek key-patterned white and gold sinks with gold and rose quartz fixtures. Beveled mirrors over the vanities are trimmed with Clarence House roping. Beneath each mirror, paintings removed from the Boudoir are mounted in plaster surrounds. Matching beveled mirrors accented with crystal sconces are positioned beside the main mirrors, opposite each other, providing an excellent reflection. Authentic reproduction Louis XV paper from Bailey & Griffin covers the walls. The Louis XV plasterwork, reproduced from the original plasterwork in the Master Bedroom, is highlighted with 23.5-karat gold leafing. The Clarence House floral patterned wallpaper matches the Clarence House-fringed Schumacher draperies framing the Master Bath's windows.

The Boudoir

The Boudoir, Claudia Uihlein's dressing room, was gutted; several of its doors were sealed off; and it was remodeled in the French theme of the entire Master Suite.

Fourteen beveled mirrored doors with crystal pulls now open to closets that cover the walls of the Boudoir. These mirrored doors also conceal a built-in marble-top vanity. Above these doors are hand-painted appliqués of flower baskets. Original floral paintings over the doors have been restored. The walls are upholstered in aubergine-colored Moire, and the windows are framed by matching silk Schumacher draperies. Forget-me-nots, favorites of Becky's mother, are woven into the border of the richly colored carpeting of the Boudoir. Above this carpeting hangs an antique Russian chandelier made of polished amethyst beads and crystal.

THE MASTER BEDROOM

The stunning, crisp details of the original ornamental plasterwork in the Master Bedroom, revealed only after artisans labored for several weeks to strip away layers of old paint, are now painted and glazed ivory and accented with 23.5-karat gold leaf.

Twelve hand-rubbed coats of varnish, lacquer, and wax were used to create the faux-painted rose quartz center panels that were installed in 15 columns around the bedroom.

A French Bell du Quin tops a queen-size sleigh bed upholstered in pink fabric from Clarence House. The Egyptian cotton bed linens are edged in an embroidered "Royal Hound" pattern by Bischoff of Switzerland.

The spectacular hand-woven carpet bears a French design, an oval floral arrangement with a medallion of colored tulips in the center. This design sets the pattern for the floor coverings throughout the suite. Woven into the borders of this carpet are forget-me-nots, peacock feathers, and intricate scrollwork. The floral border is repeated in a simpler pattern in the hallway carpet, while another oval, sans tulip medallion, is found on the Boudoir carpet.

The room is furnished with gilded and glazed Karges French reproductions. Matching end tables are antique 18th-century Italian. The lamps are antique French crystal lusters, and the chandeliers, reproductions from Neslé of New York, are lead crystal with gilded frames.

THE PRESIDENT'S SUITE

Located directly at the top of the Grand Staircase is the President's Suite. This centrally located room overlooking the reflection pool, the fountains, and the gardens of the front lawn features a large double-door balcony.

During the renovation, two built-in corner closets and a doorway leading to the Master Suite were removed to create greater privacy in both suites.

The regal carpet, hand-woven by the famed V'soske family, features fleur-de-lis and gold stars set against a deep royal blue background. The walls are upholstered in a bold striped floral French-style Clarence House fabric. The Brunschwig & Fils draperies have a bright, colorful floral motif. An Empire reproduction swan chandelier from Kings Antiques hangs elegantly in the center of the room.

The furnishings in this room include a Louis XVI rosewood-and-brass columned French Walnut armoire (circa 1850) and a large blue Schumacher fabric-covered chair and ottoman from Baker, Knapp & Tubbs. The bed has a rich gold-leafed and burgundy upholstered Karges headboard. French Empire marble and bronze lamps sit on two antique oval night tables with brown marble tops. The Italian Colombo writing desk is paired with a Karges oval-back gold-leafed armchair upholstered in a vivid striped fabric.

THE PRESIDENT'S BATHROOM

Restored to match the stately elegance of the President's Suite, the Bathroom contains a vanity designed to imitate the ornate French Walnut Louis XVI armoire in the bedroom. This walnut-and-satinwood-inlaid vanity has a rich caramel-colored Giallo Reale marble top, whose tones are picked up in the caramel and white marble floor.

The white sink with its gold Greek key design and the vanity and shower fixtures, which feature gold and lapis lazuli, are all Sherle Wagner designs. The shower is inlaid with lapis lazuli tiles. The window is framed by Indian silk with Schumacher fringe and a balloon shade. The blue damask wallpaper is from Osbourn & Little.

THE CHELSEA BEDROOM

The Chelsea Bedroom is linked to the President's Suite by the President's Bathroom. This second guest room contains much of its original paneling, which now features inlaid panels of Brunschwig & Fils French taffeta. A Regency-style antique brass chandelier and Empire sconces light the room. A tightly woven gold wool carpet covers the floor.

The Chelsea Room contains a queen-size bed and matching armoire from the Beidermier collection of Baker, Knapp & Tubbs. The bed is covered with Rose Cummings chintz featuring Mongolian warriors on horseback. Matching reproduction Louis XV black lacquer and bronze night tables flank the headboard. Other furnishings include a hand-decorated Karges chinoiserie desk, above which hangs an antique Italian baroque mirror.

THE CANOPY BEDROOM

The third guest bedroom, called the Canopy Bedroom, was originally used by one of the Uihlein staff. It was enlarged to accommodate a hand-painted ivory-colored queen-size canopy bed and a hand-painted Ethan Allen armoire.

The room is papered in a French Boussac fabric featuring a delicate floral pattern on a navy blue background. The draperies and canopy are done in a lined, polished cotton fabric featuring hot air balloons in a Chinese motif. The Baker, Knapp & Tubbs canopy bed sits between matching antique American oak harp night tables. On both of the nightstands are marble and bronze column lamps. Two matched hand-carved, silver-veneered chairs from India are displayed on the golden brown ribbed wool Belgium carpet.

THE PINK BEDROOM

I n the Pink Bedroom both the wall covering and the window treatments are done in a bold pink amaryllis in a Chinese blue vase design from Westgate Fabrics. An ivory white iron trundle bed with white eyelet bedspread and matching pillow sham is paired with white wicker furniture.

The original white plumbing fixture was replaced by a matching set of gold-trimmed, pink Ming-patterned Sherle Wagner fixtures, including a pedestal sink, faucets, towel bar and soap dish.

The cast bronze-and-porcelain chandelier, original to the room, features hanging pink porcelain rosebuds.

THE YELLOW BEDROOM

With a spectacular view of Lake Michigan from its east window, this northeast corner guest bedroom has bright yellow, white, and blue wallpaper featuring Chinese vases and plates suggesting a room decorated in wall-mounted delftware. Both the toile-covered headboard of the room's twin-size bed and the toile window treatment feature a French pastoral scene. A colorful hand-quilted, floral-patterned bedspread adorns the bed.

The room also contains a small reproduction Queen Anne drop-front desk, featuring a lighted glass cabinet above the writing table. A hand-painted blue, white, and gold chinoiserie Sherle Wagner pedestal sink, faucets, and wall-mounted soap dish and towel rack, replaced the original wall-hung sink and faucets. A tightly woven delft blue and white wool carpet covers the floor.

The room's original Venetian glass chandelier, featuring tulip stems and leaves, hangs in the center of the room.

THE CHEETAH BEDROOM

The third twin-size bedroom, the Cheetah Bedroom, is named for its cheetah-skin patterned wool carpet. The bed has a headboard covered in silk with matching draperies in a Mogul motif patterned with images of elephants, camels, and maharajas. The walls are covered in rattan-weave wallpaper in rich earth tones. Numerous pictures of Indian figures hand-painted on silk hang on the walls.

The room contains an antique dresser made of unusual burled wood veneer and an antique Indian night table with a dark wood diagonal pattern inlay. Carved brass accent lamps from India are placed on the dressers. A hand-painted, waterlily-patterned Sherle Wagner pedestal sink with gold and porcelain fixtures replaced the original wall-hung sink. Hanging from the ceiling is the room's original chandelier with its hand-painted glass globes.

THE MEDIA ROOM

A bedroom next to the Grand Staircase and overlooking Lake Michigan was converted into a Media Room that is now used as a den and reading room.

The walls of this room are upholstered in a deep blue Brunschwig & Fils French toile fabric with intricate taupe scrolls and figures. A plush armchair and ottoman are upholstered in this same fabric. Taupe Henry Calvin silk-woven fabric draperies are accented with Brunschwig & Fils fringe. The Savnik & Co. of California wool carpeting combines hand-woven and machine-woven techniques to create a simple but classic geometric pattern.

The Media Room features a large white television armoire, which houses a surround sound television system, and a pair of matching heavy brass antique chandeliers that came from another mansion on Milwaukee's eastside. These chandeliers are complemented by a pair of brass wall sconces from Design Galleries. The room's furnishings include a one-of-a-kind French Louis XVI desk, imported by Baker, Knapp & Tubbs, and a pair of round wooden tables with swan-head legs that flank a traditional sofa covered in a taupe floral-patterned damask. Brass-and-rams-horn lamps are positioned on each end table. Also featured is a handmade silver-and-enamel octagonal flower stand from India.

A refrigerator, microwave oven, and marble countertop dry bar with built-in cabinets providing storage for barware and an assortment of beverages were added.

Adjacent to the Media Room is a completely remodeled bathroom done in taupe and ivory French toile "Jeannette" wallpaper, which depicts children playing at the seashore. Seven antique hand-painted and framed lithographs of seashells adorn the walls. Chocolate brown Emporador marble was used for the floor, vanity top, and the corner shower stall, which replaced the original bathtub. The gold shower and vanity fixtures are by Sherle Wagner. An Empire period brass and crystal basket chandelier and matching brass torch sconces provide ample lighting. The room is completed with an ornate white and gold French mirror.

THE THIRD FLOOR

Originally, the third floor housed two bedrooms and a bathroom for the Uihlein boys. Later, a state-of-the-art recording studio had occupied the center of the third floor.

During the renovation, the north end was converted into a kitchenette, dining area, and art gallery. The walls of the gallery are covered with signed, limited edition prints from notable wildlife artists, including Owen Gromme, Don Moore, Don Kloetzke, Jerry Gadamus, Scott Zoellick, and Robert Abbott.

Adjacent to the kitchen is a comfortable living room and an office, which can also serve as a spare guest room. Signed and numbered prints by nostalgia artist Jim Daly decorate the walls.

A second staircase descends from the third floor all the way to the basement, providing an alternate entrance and exit.

A full bathroom with a Kohler steeping whirlpool tub, vanity, and fixtures is located near the main staircase. Its walls are covered in a green-and-white-checked Oriental-motif paper by Clarence House. The floor, shower, and whirlpool tub are bordered in white tiles accented by multicolored floral tiles and trim.

Paneled in honey-colored knotty pine, a wood used frequently in Becky's native Texas, the area west of the main staircase contains a built-in pine desk, with matching computer table and printer stand. The stairwell has built-in pine bookcases, which, along with the television cabinet and the office furniture, have been stained to match the honey-colored knotty pine paneling.

French doors were installed to provide access to a small, completely secluded porch above the portico porch, which overlooks the entire front yard.

THE LIVING ROOM

The east side of the Third Floor, now a large living room, features honey-colored leather furniture. The carpet throughout is a tightly woven honey, brown, and black wool sisal style.

Two Indian area rugs—one of hand-loomed silk, the other of wool—provide an exotic accent. Two louvered windows added to the center eastern wall, 50 feet above the ground, provide a magnificent view of Lake Michigan.

The south end of the Third Floor houses a meditation room and an exercise room. The meditation room, which is filled with icons, statues, and artifacts from many world religions, provides a retreat for personal solitude and prayer.

The exercise room is equipped with free weights, a universal gym, and the latest cardiovascular exercise equipment. Mirrors and a ballet bar are located on one wall. A ceiling-mounted television and VCR were installed to provide entertainment during workouts.

THE BILLIARDS ROOM

The Billiards Room was originally a playroom for the Uihlein children. The refinished hand-carved ribbon-and-reed mahogany fireplace mantel sets the tone for all of the woodwork in this section of the Mansion. The India earth slate floor, identical to that found in the home of Kailas's mother in India, has a soft and natural color that beautifully complements the rich mahogany paneling and woodwork.

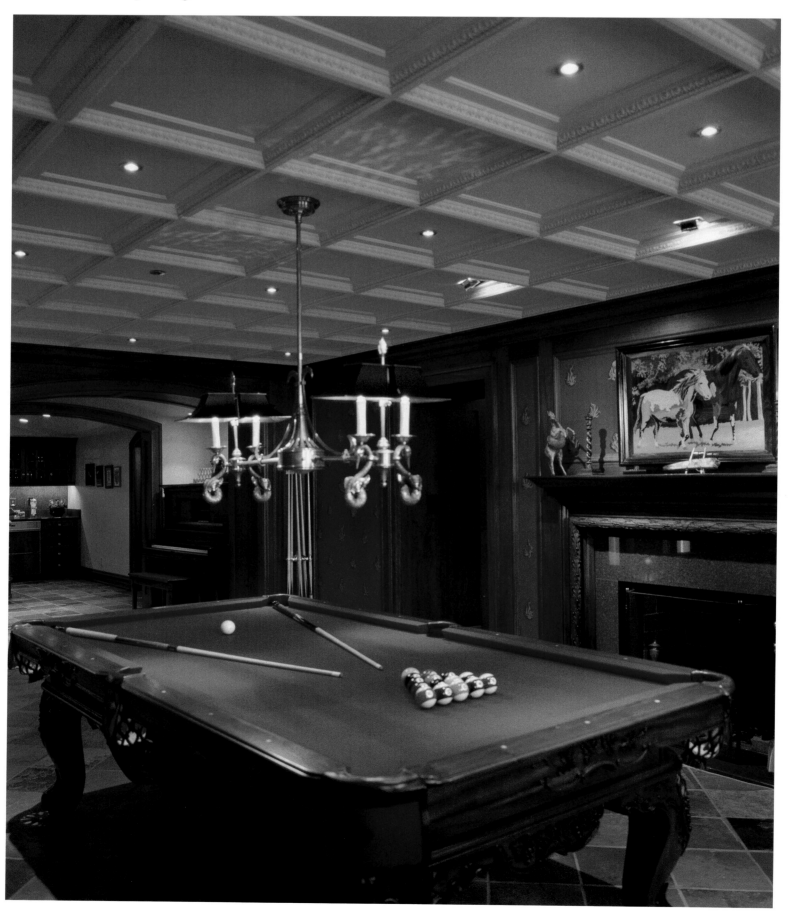

The principal furnishings of this room include a mahogany billiards table and a Wurlitzer 1056 One-More-Time coin-operated jukebox, complete with 45-rpm records featuring hits of the 50's and 60's. Six exotic wood cue sticks custom made by the McDermott Cue Company accompany the billiards table. Autographed Green Bay Packer helmets and footballs are displayed on the window ledges.

Adjoining the Billiards Room is an anteroom with a 100-year-old Aeolian player piano. This anteroom, with its barrel-vaulted ceiling, leads to a mahogany bar complete with a built-in icemaker, a microwave, a refrigerator, a brass sink and faucets, and brown-speckled granite countertops.

THE THEATER

At the south end of the lower level lies a 27-seat multimedia theater complete with stage, screen, and projection equipment. Available in this state-of-the-art entertainment center are Digital cable TV, satellite dish access, VHS video, Karaoke, AM/FM Radio, Laser Disc, DVD, and nine-speaker surround sound.

The Theater has multiple spotlights on dimmer switches as well as theater-type crystal sconces on each of the outer walls. The burgundy velvet stage drapery concealing the movie screen opens at the touch of a button. Reflecting the Mogul architecture style predominant in Kailas's native Hyderabad, the Theater has mahogany Mogul arched wall panels, each featuring an upholstered center panel covered in a Mogul design fabric from Brunschwig & Fils. Authentic burgundy velvet-covered theater seats complete the Theater.

THE WINE CELLAR

Built to accommodate 1,500 bottles of wine and champagne, the Wine Cellar is temperature and humidity controlled to ensure proper storage and aging of an extensive collection of fine wines. The Wine Cellar's red cedar racks are custom built, and its walls are coated with a special, non-odorous enamel paint specifically selected to keep unwanted odors or tastes from being absorbed through the wine bottles' corks. Adjacent to the Wine Cellar stands a custom-made wood Monk's drop-top wine desk.

THE LOWER LEVEL POWDER ROOM

Off the lower level Foyer's main staircase is a Renaissance-style mahogany and tile Powder Room, which features a cream-colored tumbled Travertine marble tile floor. The coffered ceiling is made of mahogany panels, which match those on the entry door and vanity. Burgundy-and-green-striped wallpaper, a green vanity countertop complete with Sherle Wagner brass fixtures, sink, and sconces, and green wainscoting complement the room's burgundy and turquoise glazed Spanish tile. Built-in glass shelving provides display space for a collection of small crystal, porcelain, and wooden artifacts from India.

CARETAKER'S APARTMENT, STORAGE AND SUB-BASEMENT

The center and northern end of the lower level provide ample storage space for the Raos' collection of 10 Christmas trees and decorations. On the east side, a large laundry room houses two original porcelain-over-concrete washtubs and two gas-fired furnaces. Five ground level windows provide generous natural light.

Originally, a 10,000-gallon cistern had been attached to the laundry room. Rainwater from the roof was collected in this cistern and then pumped through a honeycomb of charcoal filters into the laundry room, where this filtered water was used to wash the Uihlein family linens. During renovation, the cistern was disconnected, and the pumping equipment was removed.

The laundry room, which also serves as a grooming area for the Raos' show dogs, contains a stainless steel dog tub with a walk-up ramp, which provides easy waist-high access for dog bathing. Adjacent to the dog tub is a grooming table equipped with a professional hair dryer and grooming tools.

A small caretaker's apartment, consisting of a sitting room, a full bath, and a bedroom, is located at the south end of the lower level. For many years this apartment served as the living quarters for the Uihleins' chauffeur and gardener. The apartment has been carpeted, wallpapered and furnished; its bathroom has been remodeled using white French ceramic tile, rose-motif wallpaper, and new Kohler plumbing fixtures, including a scalloped pedestal sink.

Also accessible from the end of the lower level hall is a stairwell that leads to the sub-basement, where additional utilities, two commercial-size water heaters, a hot water boiler, and a furnace are housed. Because the boiler was once fired by coal, this space contains bins large enough to store two train cars of coal. These coal bins have been sealed off and filled.

THE GROUNDS OF THE ESTATE

As part of the renovation, the grounds surrounding the Mansion were completely landscaped. Great care was taken to preserve as many of the oak and maple trees from the original estate as possible.

On the west side of the Mansion is the 90-foot reflecting pool with its English lead fountains and water cannons. Specially designed for this setting, the white marble garden furniture, hand-carved in Agra, India by artisans whose ancestors built the Taj Mahal, is situated at either end of the pool. Viewed from the main gates, the house calls to mind the splendor of the grand European mansions.

The eastern side, a park-like setting of terraces, formal gardens, rose gardens and lawns, offers a stunning view of Lake Michigan. The bluff and slope down to the lakeshore were entirely rebuilt and stabilized during the renovation. A gradual transition from the formal gardens in the backyard to the winding pathway with its wild flowers, trees, and shrubs to the natural wooded shoreline and lake far below completes the restoration.

Enclosing the estate is a black iron fence installed by Munson Fence. Along Lake Drive are two sets of wrought-iron gates mounted on limestone columns.

The coach lamps mounted at the gates, on the balustrade, and on the garage were hand-wrought by Dan Nauman of Bighorn Forge. The fencing, gates, pilasters, and coach lamps are identical to those found on the original 1916 blueprints of the Mansion property.

SHARING A MASTERPIECE

The Herman and Claudia Uihlein Mansion is a special place-a home to Kailas and Becky Rao and an architectural gem from Kirchoff & Rose. This Mansion stands as a monument to a great European heritage that is well represented by those artists, craftsmen, engineers, and laborers who created it and those who recreated it 80 years later.

From its original construction by the Uihleins to its complete restoration by the Raos, the Mansion has been and remains historically relevant yet thoroughly modern; elegantly grand yet decidedly down-to-earth; and highly sophisticated yet firmly rooted in this southeastern Wisconsin community. It has never been a museum but has always been a home.

Thanks to the Uihleins' original vision and the Raos' careful restoration, the Mansion is once again accomplishing its purpose: it serves as a testament to craftsmanship, as a splendid example of Italian Renaissance architecture, and as a grand and elegant meeting place, where the Raos entertain their family and friends, and where they host events for various organizations within their community, including the Milwaukee Symphony, the Boys and Girls Clubs of Greater Milwaukee, The Children's Hospital of Wisconsin, and UNICEF.

Boys and Girls Club Jazz Band

Marty Stein, Jim Ericson

Jack McKeithan, Kailas and Doc Severinsen

*Governor and Mrs. Tommy Thompson,
Kailas and Becky Rao*

Dave Mancini

Lorry Uihlein, Mr. and Mrs. Don Schuenke

Tom and Darla Ament, Dick Steinman

Henry Ferguson, Gerald Zadikoff, Vickie Livingston

Prema Gelli, Jane Dicus

Bill Dicus, Julie and Mason Ross

Jim and Janet McKenna, Dick and Joan Abdoo

Bronson and Jackie Haase, Kailas Rao

Dick and Ellen Glaisner, Haresh and Meena Patel

Fred and Anne Stratton, Kailas Rao

Herman and Pam Viets, the Raos

Howard and Barbara Schnoll, Kailas Rao

Doc and Emily Severinsen, Kailas and Becky Rao,
Joel DiBartola, Liz Story

George and Pauline Dalton, the Raos

Becky Rao, Marco Steiger, Rocco Finizio

Margie and Greg Larson, Gowri and Shobha Kailas,
Mohan Kailas, Dr. Katta

The Raos, Dan Hesse

Fred Luber, the Raos, Dona and Tom Miotke

Terry O'Reilly, Lori Krezwinski

Linda Steffans Williams

133

Don and Rosemarie Brier

Josie Simmons, Beverly Bast

Cathy and Stan Litwin, Don Myles, Chris Litwin, Kailas Rao

John and Rosio Yousif, Kathy O'Reilly

Jorge and Sofija Galante, Joanne Friedman

Judge Leo and Doris Whinery, Becky Rao

Lupe and Dan King

Bill and Jane Dicus, Prema Gelli, Becky Rao

Paul Cox, Rick Kinder, Friends from Alcatel

Janice Tishberg, Becky Rao, Lucy Newman,
Arlene Newman

Diane Steuernagel, Jim and Nancy Papandrea

The Raos. Sue Moglia, Venus Hurtado-Cote

Sudha and Ramakrisha Velamati, the Raos

Kanti and Sarada Prasad, the Raos

Becky and Kailas Rao, Doc Severinsen,
Tom and Chris Shewczyk

Bill and Linda Abraham, Terry Kennedy, Predeep Kaul

"Larry the Legend" and Mary Johnson

Amy Stillman Anderson, Kimberly Stillman,
Sharon Stillman

Paul, Vikki, Tammi and Eric Cox

The Shelley Family Reunion

Beth and Kevin Burger and Rhianna

Kailas Rao's Family Reunion

Vic and Lou Sanders, Jess Daniels, Barbara Rodgers,
Beverly Burger, Lynn Allison, Becky Rao

Girish and Niraj Gelli

Christine and Al Salamone, Paul and Sara Callahan, Lisa Salamone

Kailas Rao's Family Reunion

Laxman and Sujatha, Kailas Rao

Doc Severinsen, Chris Salamone

Lee and Doug Linnemann, Andrew Linnemann, Beverly Burger, the Raos

Becky Rao, Jill and Clint Daniels

Kailas Rao's nieces and nephews

Easwar Ajit, the Raos, Mr. C. Kandoor

137

Susan and Chris DeChant

Venkanna and Rukmini Kanna, Vani and Nick Ott,
Rekha and Sanjay Abell

The Raos, Alan "Bud" Selig

Gowri, Sri Ramlu, Mohan, Kailas Rao, Laxman

Laxman, Don and Lyn Kennedy, Kailas Rao,
Mike and Debbie Flannigan

Sunny Mehta and Cori

Carolyn Dicus

Wendy Selig Prieb, Kailas Rao

The Raos, Renata and Alberto Stein,
Girish Gelli, Skyler

Rick and Debra Kinder, the Raos,
Jerry and Gwen Berlin

ACKNOWLEDGMENTS

So many people have helped us with the creation and preparation of this book and with the actual restoration of the Herman and Claudia Uihlein Mansion that we are bound to forget to thank all of the numerous people who contributed to the book project and to the restoration project, so let us begin with an apology to those we may have overlooked and with a hearty thank you.

Of those involved with the book project, we are most grateful to our dear friend Art Hastings. He inspired us to tackle this project and was the glue that held it together. Art's magnificent photographs, expressive text, enthusiasm, and dedication are the heart—the very big heart—of this project. Tragically, Art passed away in 2000 before the completion of this book. He devoted countless hours of his time not only to this book but also to us, as our friend and colleague. Our lives are greatly enriched for our having known Art. We will always remember him with tremendous fondness and respect. We would also like to thank Phyllis, Art's wife, and their children, Michael and Kristen, for their help.

We are also particularly grateful to Mary Uihlein Cunningham and Nancie and Herman Uihlein, Jr., who so generously shared their time, photographs, and invaluable information regarding the history of their family.

Special thanks are also due to Laxman Kailas, who not only did much of the research on the Mansion as it was being restored but also photographed the restoration process.

We would also like to thank Michael Lyons for his creative direction in the design and production of this book. Michael's artistic sensibilities and zeal for perfection complement the effort of those who brought the mansion back to its original splendor.

We are also immensely grateful to the following people: Dick Glaisner, who provided us with just the right balance of encouragement, counsel, and caution when we approached him with our idea to purchase the Mansion; Peter and Mary Buffet, who in accepting our offer, graciously passed on to us the ownership of this magnificent house; and Donald and Donna Baumgartner, who willingly shared the insight and information they had gained from carrying out their own extensive remodeling project and who generously introduced us to those who would become our restoration project team.

The restoration of the Mansion was the work of many heads, hearts, and hands. Our deepest acknowledgments go to Greg Pardo and Jon Schlagenhaft, who adeptly led the restoration project from start to finish and whose valuable and expert opinion made it possible for us to fulfill our vision for the Mansion.

Additionally, we would like to express special gratitude to all those individuals who were part of the project from the beginning and who were instrumental in moving it successfully throughout its various stages: Ron Buchert, Ron Michels, Bob and John Hosni, Dave North, Paul Casey, Bob Erdmann, David J. Frank, Steve Balasch, Don Soderberg, Jim Mitchrich, Charley Brown, Mark Evans, and Erv Huber.

We would also like to extend our appreciation to the following people to whom we are greatly indebted for their help in various ways: Christine Salamone, Agnes Dolecki, and Susan Pardo.

Kailas and Becky Rao

TESTIMONIALS

"Our family has appreciated seeing the home restored to its original splendor. It has been such a wonderful thing for our grandchildren to see this part of the legacy of their grandparents, Herman and Claudia Uihlein, brought to life."
Nancie Uihlein

"Everyone was so pleased and surprised to see our old home become alive again. I know the work and effort that was put into your home as I was one of the lucky ones to see it on its way."
Mary Uihlein Cunningham

"My grandparents [Herman and Claudia Uihlein] would be proud of the house's restoration and pleased that it is being shared by Becky and Kailas Rao for others to enjoy."
Peter Uihlein

"...[H]ow good it was to see the house, in all of its newfound beauty, awash in light and laughter."
Polly and Henry Uihlein

"What Kailas and Becky have done with the house is absolutely spectacular...the home is the epitome of grand style."
Mrs. Lorry Uihlein

"I appreciated the great care you used to restore the house to its original grandeur while at the same time incorporating your own personalities and experiences. Thank you for your generosity in sharing your home with the community."
Scott McCallum,
former Governor of Wisconsin

"The work you have done to restore the home is breathtaking."
Tom Barrett,
former U.S. Congressman for Wisconsin

"I would like to thank you for your generous contribution to Milwaukee's architectural history... Were it not for your interest and dedication, this spectacular mansion would be all but lost—history, so to speak."
Mike Jacobs,
newscaster, Channel 4 (WTMJ)

"[T]hank you for your great generosity in opening your palazzo as a benefit for the Orchestra this weekend. You have doubly benefited our community by your monumental investment in the restoration/improvement of your home and your support of our world-class orchestra."
Edwin P. Wiley,
President, Milwaukee Symphony Orchestra

"Approaching Becky and Kailas Rao's striking home at the holidays is a magical experience.... Every beautifully appointed room has its own warm and impeccable character, including countless unique holiday trimmed trees to celebrate the season."
Victoria Wellens,
Executive Director, Wisconsin Humane Society

"Walking into the mansion...one experiences the glory of history past restored today. It is much more than simply seeing a museum to the past. It is an experience in living in wonder and glory of both past and present."
Pastor Richard Jones,
United Methodist Church of Whitefish Bay

"I have come to know that the restoration of the Rao residence is not only one of amazing faithfulness to the original house but a restoration of the spirit as well. A place of generosity, good works for the community, and loving attitudes for all who enter there."
Doc Severinsen, Principal Conductor,
Milwaukee Symphony Pops Orchestra

"The home of Kailas & Becky Rao has a special place in the hearts and minds of all...associated with the Boys & Girls Clubs of Greater Milwaukee. Their premiere residence has made the Raos two of Milwaukee's most gracious hosts."
Thomas L. Spero, Chairman of the Board,
Boys & Girls Clubs of Greater Milwaukee 2001-2003

"[The Raos] took a building that had once been lovingly created but that had fallen into disrepair and not only revived and reconstructed it, but gave it new life and luster. It is a superb job and one that honors not only the early twentieth-century building but its present owners and occupants."
Henry Ferguson

"I will always have fond memories of the house. It created an atmosphere that allowed me to write a number of pieces of music, including the Firedance scene in 'Dances With Wolves' and the song '(Searching For) A Place Called Home.'"
Peter Buffett

"From the beauty of the reflecting pool on a summer evening to the breathtaking lake views from the house's balconies to the sheer elegance of the house itself, the Raos' home is truly majestic and is probably one of the finest I've ever been in.... [D]espite its majesty and elegance, it exudes the warmth and spirit of a loving home."
George Dalton, Chairman,
CEO, & Founder, Call Solutions

"In the spring of 1993, Kailas came to me with the idea of purchasing a wonderful Lake Drive home and restoring it to its original condition. I suggested to Kailas that purchasing the property was the easy part; the restoration would take a tremendous amount of time, patience and perseverance to say the least. Undaunted, Becky and Kailas "jumped in" much further than I could have imagined, and the final result is a tribute to our city, its artisans and our wonderful history."

> Dick Glaisner, Senior Vice President of Wealth
> Management, Wells Fargo Bank, Milwaukee

"As someone who has undertaken a significant remodeling project on an estate, I can fully appreciate the tremendous work and thought the Raos have put into the spectacular restoration of their magnificent home. I commend Greg Pardo, John Schlagenhaft, Ron Buchert, Bob Hosni, and all of our team who worked on this project for a job superbly done, and I congratulate the Raos on their elegant and beautifully restored home."

> Donald Baumgartner, President,
> Paper Machine Company

"I love what Kailas and Becky have done with the old Uihlein mansion. The house has such interesting detail—something you just don't see in houses built in more recent times. Kailas and Becky took the time to restore the house and its detail carefully so that we as well as they can enjoy it. I thank them for preserving this part of Milwaukee's history."

> Fred Stratton, Chairman & CEO, Briggs & Stratton

"The magnificent renovation and landscape design at your Whitefish Bay home has truly demonstrated your commitment to historical preservation and old-world craftsmanship. The historical significance of the Cyril Colnik grand staircase is priceless to our community and would not have been possible without your long-term dedication and love of this beautiful residence."

> Patti and Jack McKeithan,
> President, Tamarack Petroleum Company, Inc.

"This labor of love in restoring the former Uihlein property to its past grandeur is deeply appreciated by all. The Raos' opening of their home for numerous charitable and civic development events, such as The Diabetes Foundation and Milwaukee Children's Hospital, reaffirms their love of Milwaukee. "

> Terrence M. O'Reilly,
> Executive Vice-President, Call Solutions

"You have done a spectacular remodeling to make your home a national showpiece."

> Anne and Fred Luber, Chairman,
> Super Steel Corporation

"What you have done is nothing short of incredible. It is clear that you are committed to the future of this area but realize that the past is equally important. Future generations owe a debt of gratitude to you for preserving this landmark home."

> Keith Miller, President, M/Barrington

"While one finds much to admire in a house as grand and impressive as the Raos', the generous and welcoming attitudes of the owners, reflected in the home, set this mansion apart from many others. Despite their historical accuracy, Becky and Kailas have incorporated their own unique taste and generous personalities into the refurbishing."

> Bill, Jane, and Carolyn Dicus

"[T]hank you for what you have done on behalf of Milwaukee's heritage. Your home will be preserved for generations for all to see and enjoy."

> John Stollenwerk, President/CEO,
> Allen Edmonds Shoe Corporation

"You have done a wonderful thing in rebuilding your home… [Y]our efforts can be seen as a service to all of us, because you are preserving a piece of history."

> Hermann Viets, President,
> Milwaukee School of Engineering

"The time and effort (not to mention expense) involved in a restoration of this magnitude and accuracy must have been enormous, albeit a labor of love…. [Y]ou have used the home so generously, sharing it with the community in numerous important ways, such as the recent meeting for Children's Hospital."

> William J. Abraham, Jr., Partner,
> Foley & Lardner, Attorneys at Law

"Arlene and I remember looking at purchasing the house…. It didn't occur to us to turn the renovation into a labor of love and restore the house to its original grandeur. You and Becky did…. The community is the recipient of a piece of its history that it can view in as close to its original state as possible."

> Joel S. Lee, President, Van Buren Management

"The meticulous restoration of the Uihlein Mansion to its original splendor…has helped preserve a wonderful symbol of Wisconsin's heritage. As if this is not enough, the continued use of their gracious home to help promote a variety of charitable causes is a tribute to the profound community-mindedness of the Raos."

> Dr. Anita and Dr. Prem Sharma,
> former Dean of Marquette University Dental School,
> and author of *Mandalay's Child*

"A true privilege to walk through the doors of this beautifully restored Milwaukee treasure. One feels echoes of the "sound of music" era when you enter the gates–every detail exquisite in its elegance, history, and charm. A trip back in time."

> Sue and Dick Steinman

RESTORATION PROJECT TEAM

INTERIOR DESIGNER

JON SCHLAGENHAFT DESIGN, LTD.

PROJECT MANAGER

GREGORY PARDO

ARTISANS & CRAFTSMEN

Affiliated Artists
American Seating
Balasch Painting and Decorating, Inc.
Baumeister Associates Paint Contractors
Bellkool Co.
Bighorn Forge
BJ Weather-stripping Co.
Ronald Buchert- General Contractor Carpentry
Paul Casey Architectural Specialties
Cedar Disposal
Childcrest Tile and Stone
Classic Garden Ornaments Ltd.
Classic Lamps
Conrad Schmitt Studios, Inc.
Designer's Workroom, Inc.
Dittrich Engineering Inc.
Robert Doctor
Engberg-Anderson Consulting
Environmental Material Disposal Services
Lawrence A. Ernest, P.E.
Evans and Brown
F & F Security Company
Al Felch Woodcarver
Fiber-Seal of Milwaukee, Inc.
The Finial
Fitness Works
The Flower Studio Ltd
David J. Frank Landscape Contracting, Inc.
Edward E. Gillen Co.
Gary Granrath Plastering
Haasch Appliances
Henricksen Office Interiors
Heritage Flooring Inc.
HiTech Homes, Inc.
Hosni Electric
Ianelli's Custom Shoppe
J and K Trucking

J.P. Marble & Tile
J. T. Roofing
Kapur & Associates
Kashou Co. Inc.
Kowalske Brothers
The Lamp Shader
Lappin Lighting Inc.
Linear Rubber Products, Inc.
Lippert Tile Company, Inc.
George Majeskie Inc.
McDermott Cue Manufacturing
Ron Michels Plumbing, Inc.
Milwaukee Marble
James Mitschrich
Munson Fence Co.
Newman Pools
David North Roofing
North Shore Marble
Painted Finishes
Percy's Linens
Quarra Stone Company, Inc.
Rickmeyer Floor Covering Inc.
Ritter Fabrication
Sage Upholstery Workroom
Robert S. Schley
Schlitz Handwrought Studios
Don Soderberg Painting
Stoetzel Video Productions
StoryBook Forge
Thomas Furniture Refinishing
VerHalen, Inc.—The Pella Window Store
Watson-Smith
George Watts and Son
The Wenninger Company, Inc.
Wisconsin Shower Door
R.D. Woods Co.
World of Wood, Ltd.